# how to CODE a sandcastle

P9-AFH-391

by **Josh Funk**

illustrated by **Sara Palacios**

foreword by Reshma Saujani, founder of Girls Who Code

SCHOLASTIC INC.

## FOREWORD

Hi, I'm Reshma, and I'm the founder of Girls Who Code.

Do you know what coding is? As you'll discover in this book, it's basically how humans tell a computer—or a robot—what to do. But it's also about using creativity and imagination to define, explore, and solve problems of all kinds.

Girls Who Code is an organization that wants to teach every girl to learn to code! And you don't have to wait until middle school or later to introduce girls to coding. Just like kids begin to learn about subjects like animals, history, and space before they get to kindergarten, we want to make coding a familiar part of every child's world. By introducing the core concepts of coding to children now, we're helping prepare them for a future of changing the world through code.

Happy reading—and coding!

*Reshma Saujani*

Hello, World, I'm Pearl.

It's the last day of summer vacation.
Which means today is my very last chance
to build a sandcastle!

I've tried every single day,
but something always ruins it!

First came the
flying saucers.

Then the shark attack.

And maybe worst of all was the moat that Ada Puglace added.

But today, I've got the perfect plan. I've brought my trusty rust-proof robot, Pascal.

He'll do whatever I tell him—as long as I tell him in CODE. It's not a *secret code*—it's special instructions that computers understand.

Hmm. I guess he doesn't know how to do that. But a coder takes one *big* problem and breaks it into several *smaller* ones. If I give Pascal enough instructions that he *does* know, we'll build this castle in no time! It'll be easy!

I guess I need to be very specific with my instructions.

Pascal, find a flat spot on sand that isn't too close to the water.

This isn't as easy as I thought.
But at least we have a place to build.

# SMALL PROBLEM #2: GATHER UP SAND

Now we'll need a *huge* pile of sand.
It's *very* important to tell Pascal everything in the correct SEQUENCE—
that means in the right order.

1. Fill the pail with sand.

2. Dump the sand on our spot.

3. Pat the sand down.

Great job, Pascal! Now let's do it again.

There must be a coding trick I can use.
Aha! A LOOP!
When you need to repeat something in code,
you can use a LOOP!

Let's each find some fancy decorations and bring them back here.

Maybe I need to give him better instructions. An IF-THEN-ELSE should do the trick.

IF the item you see is small and doesn't move and doesn't belong to anyone

THEN bring the item back to the castle

ELSE find something different

Perfect! Let's shape the castle and decorate.

A moat would have protected the castle from the tide! If only I had thought of a moat earlier. It took half the day to figure out how to **CODE** a sandcastle . . .

But hold on. I already wrote the **CODE** to build a sandcastle. I can easily use all that **CODE** again!

1. Find a place to build.

I think a new **SEQUENCE** should solve this small problem. And I know how to write one of those. Let's try:

1. Dig around the outside of the castle.

2. Fill the pail with sand.

3. Empty the pail away from the castle.

And we need to repeat that until we've gone all around the castle. I know—another LOOP!

Hurray! Our sandcastle is finished and safe from the ocean! Let's play!

Hey, Pascal, now that we know how to CODE one sandcastle . . .

We can code an entire KINGDOM!

`return(); // THE END`

```
for each (girl_n in AllGirls), StartLoop:
    print ("This book is for ", girl_n, NewLine);
:EndLoop
```

—J.F.

To the girls who code and the girls who draw.

—S.P.

No part of this publication may be reproduced, stored in a retrieval system, or transmitted in any form or by any means, electronic, mechanical, photocopying, recording, or otherwise, without written permission of the publisher. For information regarding permission, write to Viking Children's Books, an imprint of Penguin Young Readers Group, a division of Penguin Random House LLC, 1745 Broadway, New York, NY 10019.

ISBN 978-1-338-54690-3

Text copyright © 2018 by Josh Funk. Illustrations copyright © 2018 by Sara Palacios. All rights reserved. Published by Scholastic Inc., 557 Broadway, New York, NY 10012, by arrangement with Viking Children's Books, an imprint of Penguin Young Readers Group, a division of Penguin Random House LLC. SCHOLASTIC and associated logos are trademarks and/or registered trademarks of Scholastic Inc.

The publisher does not have any control over and does not assume any responsibility for author or third-party websites or their content.

12 11 10 9 8 7 6 5 4 3 2                    22 23 24

Printed in the U.S.A.                                        40

First Scholastic printing, May 2019

The illustrations for this book were rendered digitally in combination with gouache and acrylic paintings.

# Pearl and Pascal's Guide to Coding

## WHAT IS CODE?

Code is the set of instructions a computer uses to do any type of task, such as solving a problem.

Sometimes these tasks and problems can seem really big, so one thing coders do is break difficult big problems into smaller, easier ones. Rather than build an entire sandcastle, which is a difficult big task, Pearl decided to think of it as several smaller, easier tasks.

## WHAT IS A SEQUENCE?

Code must be written in a specific order called a sequence. Just like a story wouldn't make sense if the sentences were rearranged in the wrong order, code won't work if it's written in the wrong sequence.

For example, if a story is told as follows:
> Pearl wakes up.
> Pearl eats breakfast.
> Pearl gets dressed.
> Pearl goes to school.

That makes perfect sense.

However, if the order of the sentences is changed:
> Pearl eats breakfast.
> Pearl wakes up.
> Pearl goes to school.
> Pearl gets dressed.

The story no longer makes sense (and introduces many questions: Does Pearl eat breakfast in her sleep? Does she go to school in her pajamas?).

# Pearl and Pascal's Guide to Coding

## WHAT IS A LOOP?

One common coding technique is a loop. A loop helps when you want to repeat a sequence. Instead of writing the sequence over and over again, you write it only once—inside of a loop.

## WHAT IS AN IF-THEN-ELSE?

An if-then-else is sort of like answering a *true or false* question. If the answer is true, then you do one thing. If it's false, you do something else. Sometimes this is called a *conditional*.

In the story, Pascal keeps finding inappropriate decorations. Pearl uses an if-then-else to get Pascal to check whether the item is okay before bringing it back. If the item fits Pearl's rules, then Pascal can bring it back. Otherwise, Pascal will keep looking for something else.

During the day, JOSH FUNK writes C++, Java code, and Python scripts as a software engineer, which he's been doing for the last twenty years. In his spare time he uses ABC's, drinks Java coffee, and writes picture books such as *Lady Pancake & Sir French Toast*, *The Case of the Stinky Stench*, *Dear Dragon*, and more.

SARA PALACIOS has illustrated several picture books including *'Twas Nochebuena* and the Pura Belpré honor book *Marisol McDonald Doesn't Match*. She lives in San Francisco with her husband.

GIRLS WHO CODE is a national nonprofit organization working to close the gender gap in technology and change the image of what a programmer looks like and does. By the end of the 2018 academic year, Girls Who Code will have reached over fifty thousand girls in all fifty states and several US territories.